At the Beach

S M Coloring and Shading Books

A different type of coloring book, "S M Coloring and Shading Books" can be as challenging or as simple to color as you wish. The pictures are sketch-like and intentionally printed lighter, so that you can color over the gray.

For a more challenging experience, use the gray shading in the picture as a guide to work on shading techniques. We like to color over or outline the darker areas with one or a few shades of a color, then color the lighter areas with a contrasting or lighter shade.

For a simple coloring experience just color the picture, the gray may show through depending on what you are coloring with and your technique, this will give some depth to the picture. You can always outline in black if you prefer that look.

Visit our Facebook page "S M Coloring and Shading Books" for examples, ideas, techniques and more.

The pages are one-sided to enable you to take a picture out if needed for technique, framing, or a gift and not miss out on coloring the other side or have it bleed through.

Be sure to check out our whole line, search "S M Coloring and Shading Books".

Copyright © 2015   S M Coloring and Shading Books

Beach

Beach

Beach Balls

Beach Glass

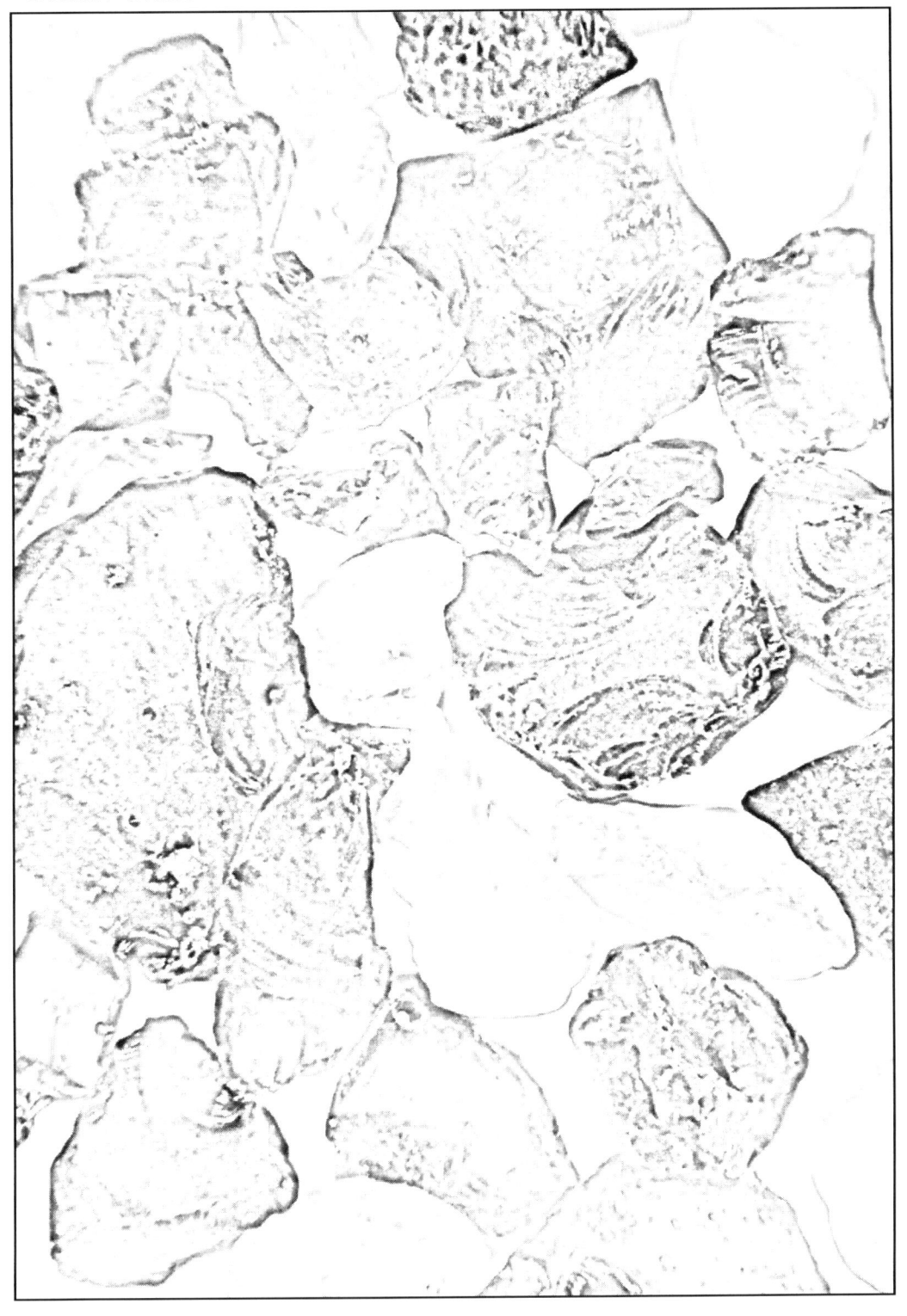

Beach Hats

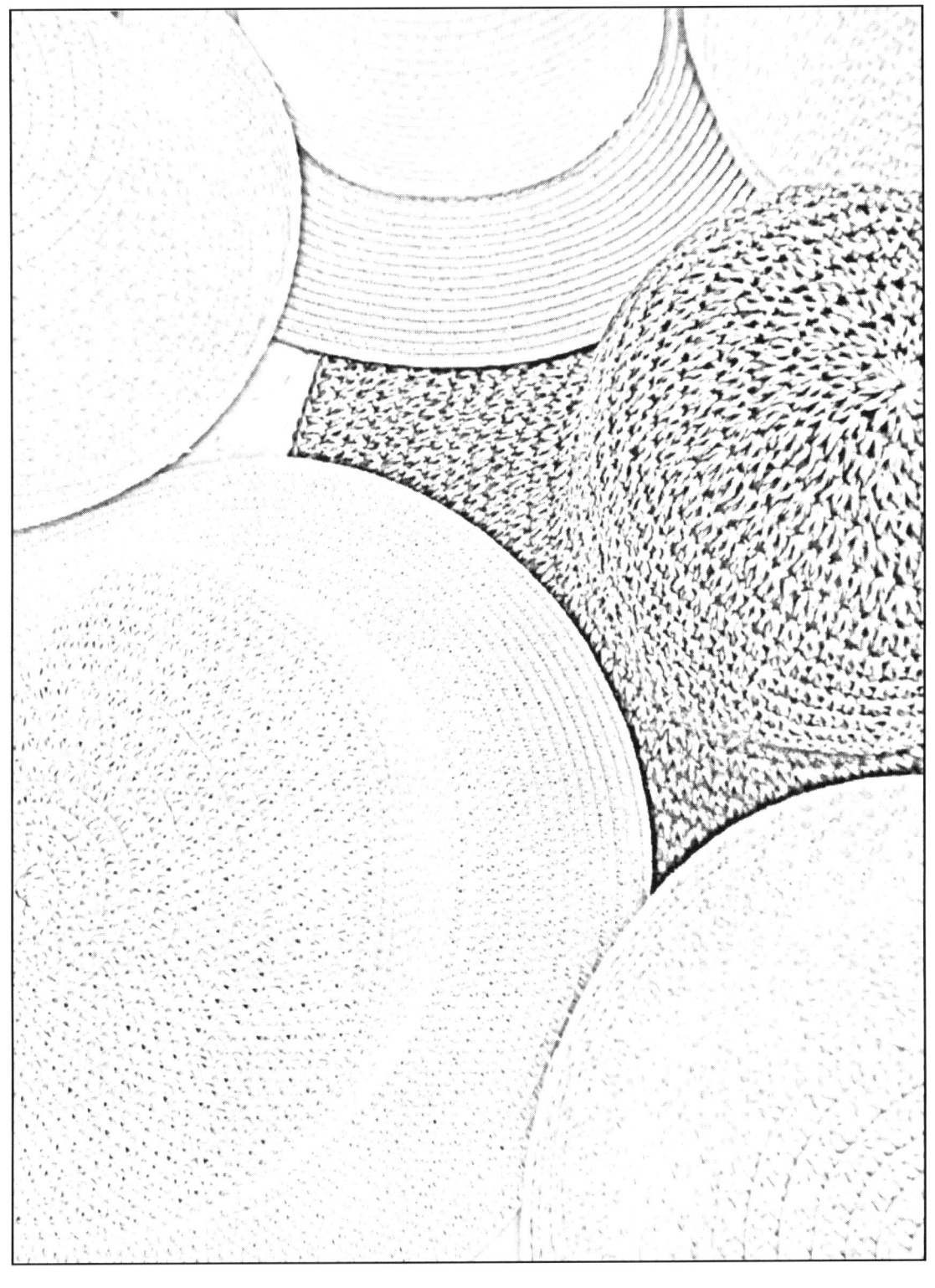

Beach Towels

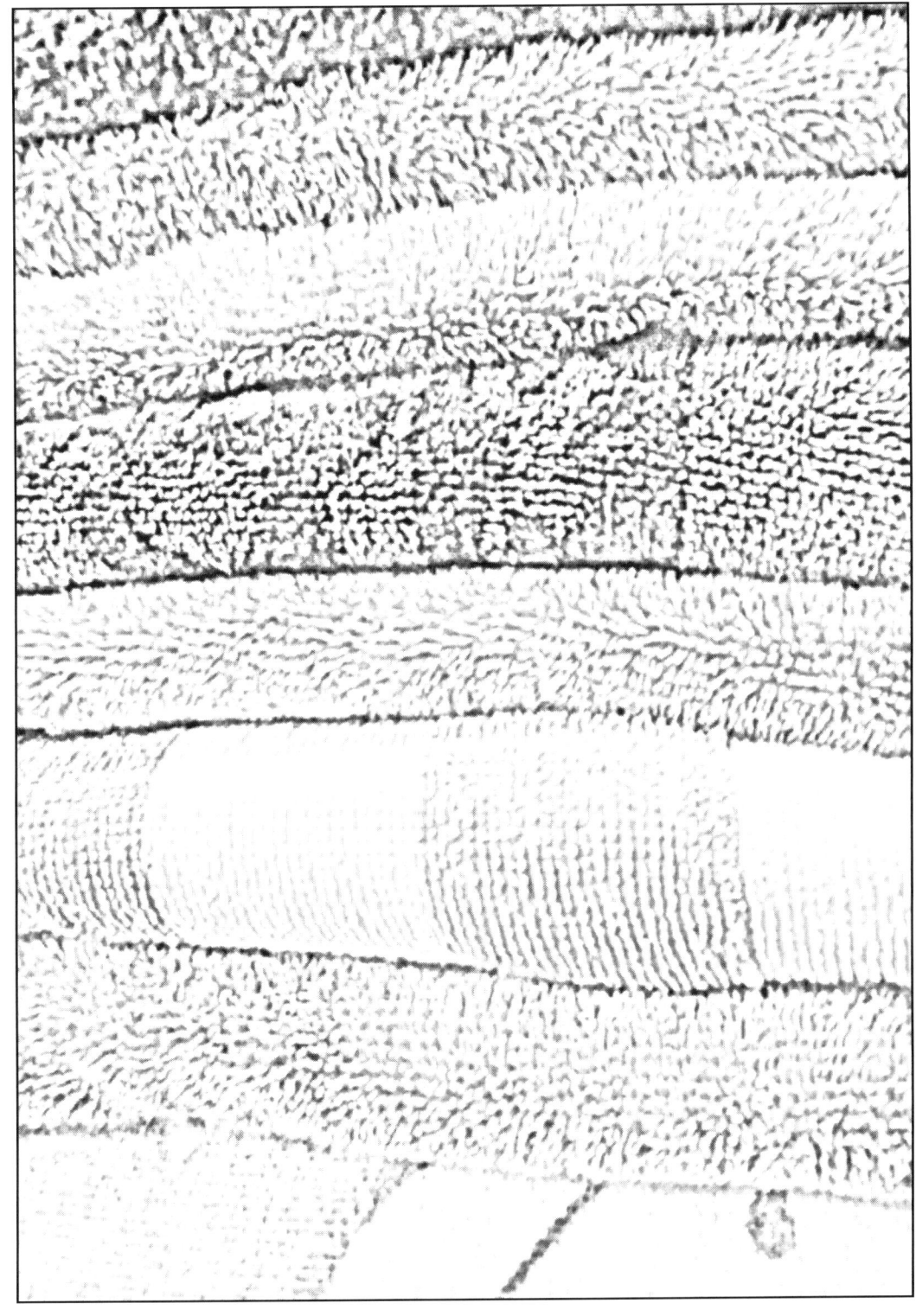

Beach Umbrellas

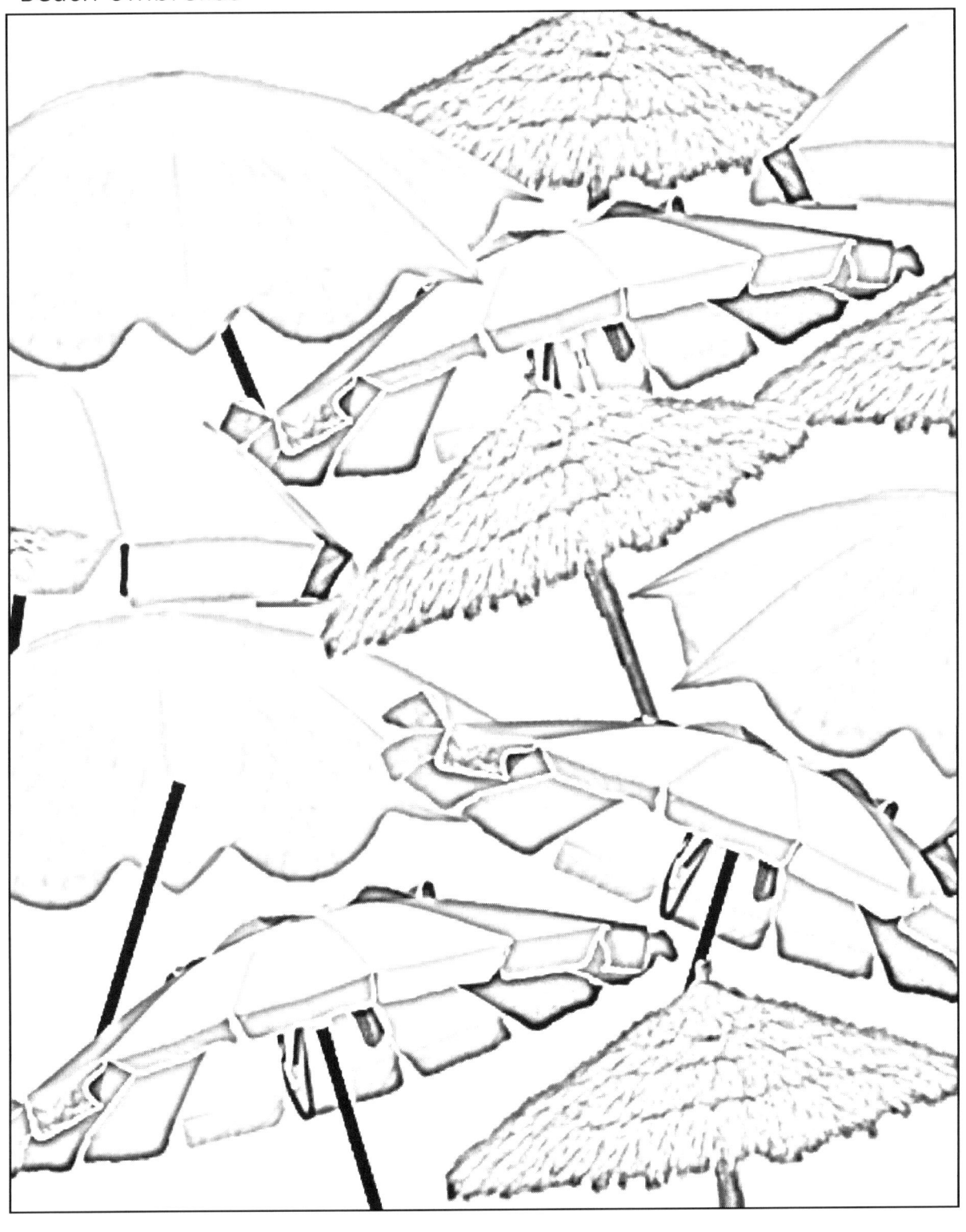

Boardwalk

Boats

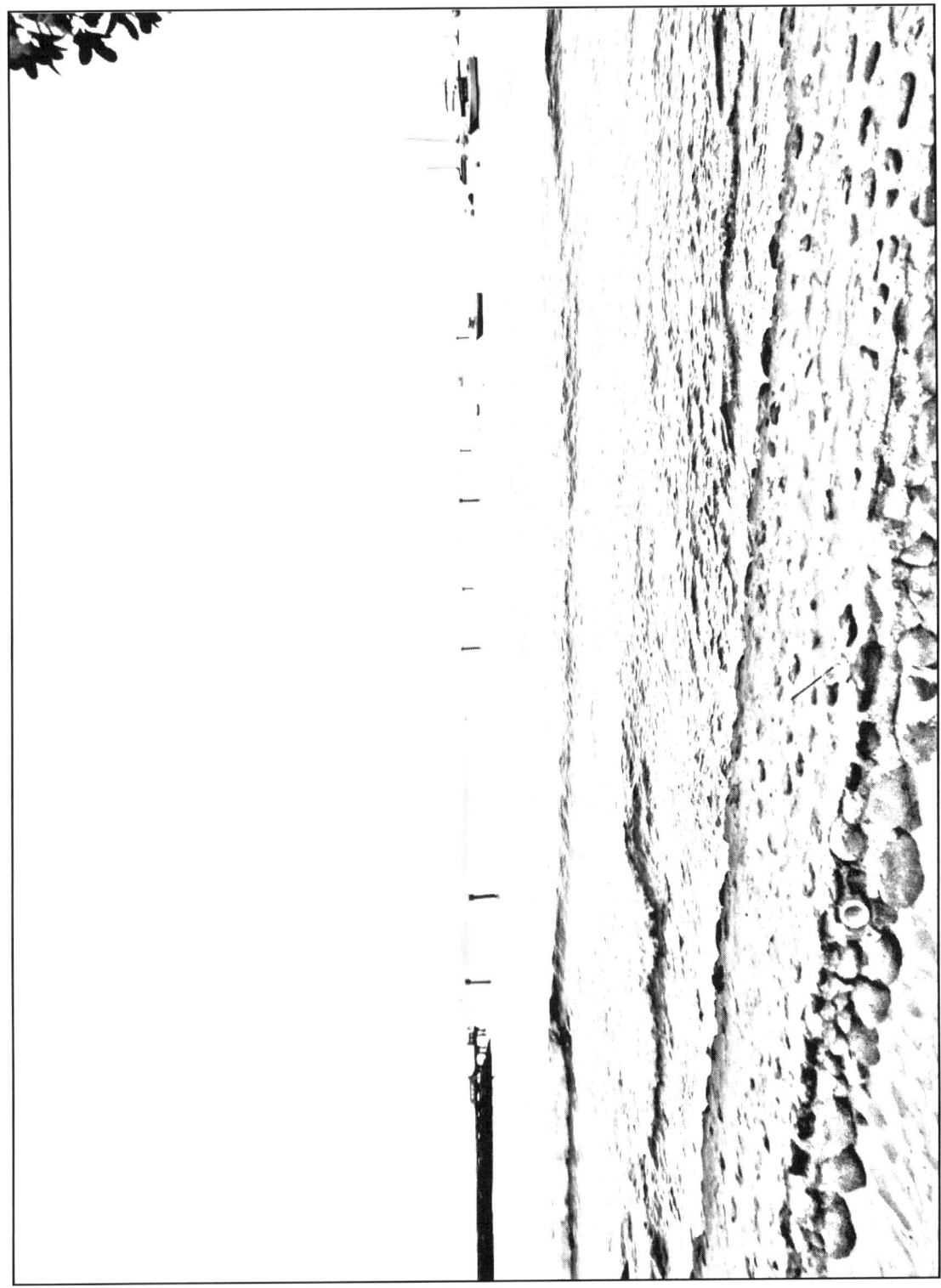

Clownfish and Anemone

Fins

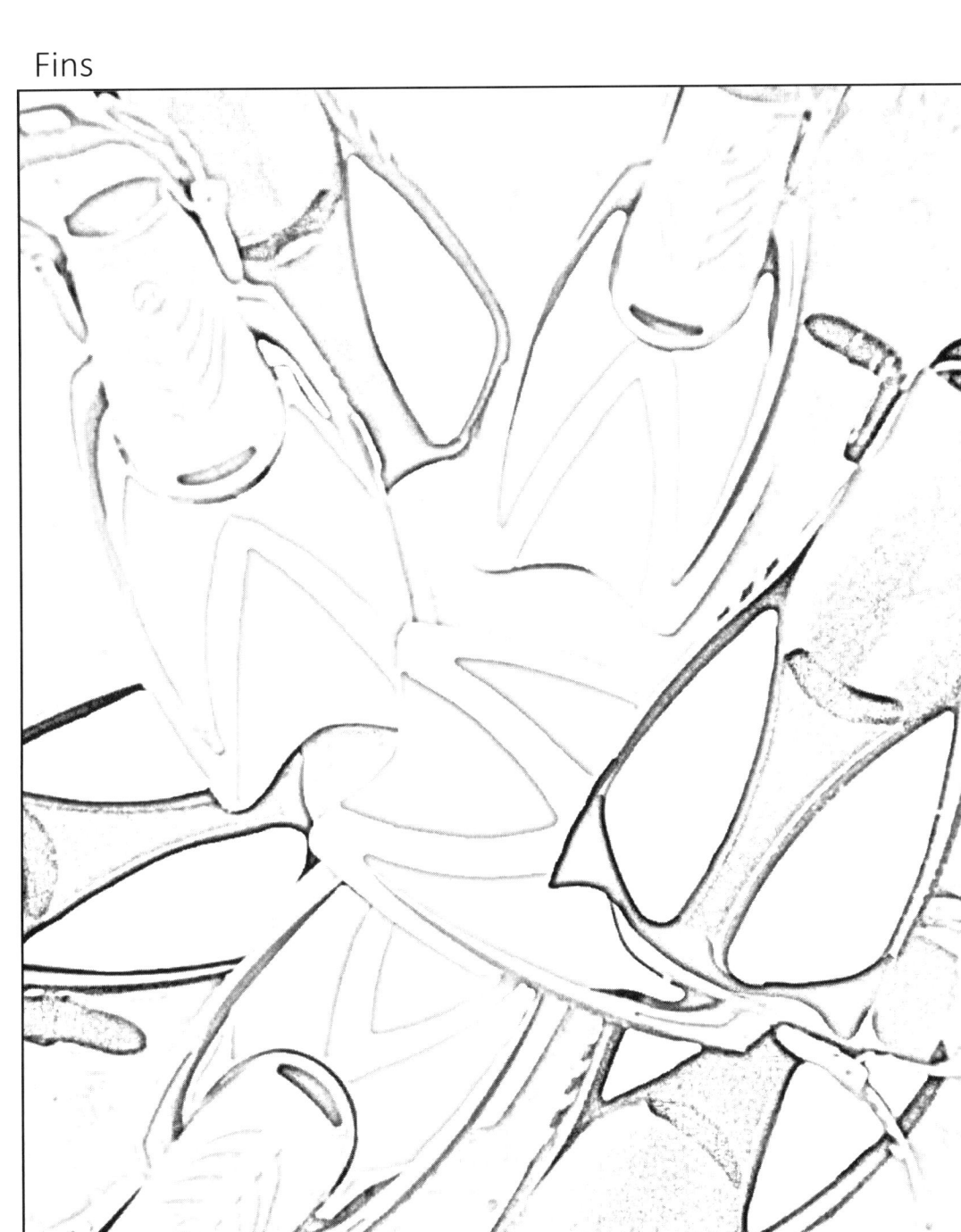

Fish

Flip Flops

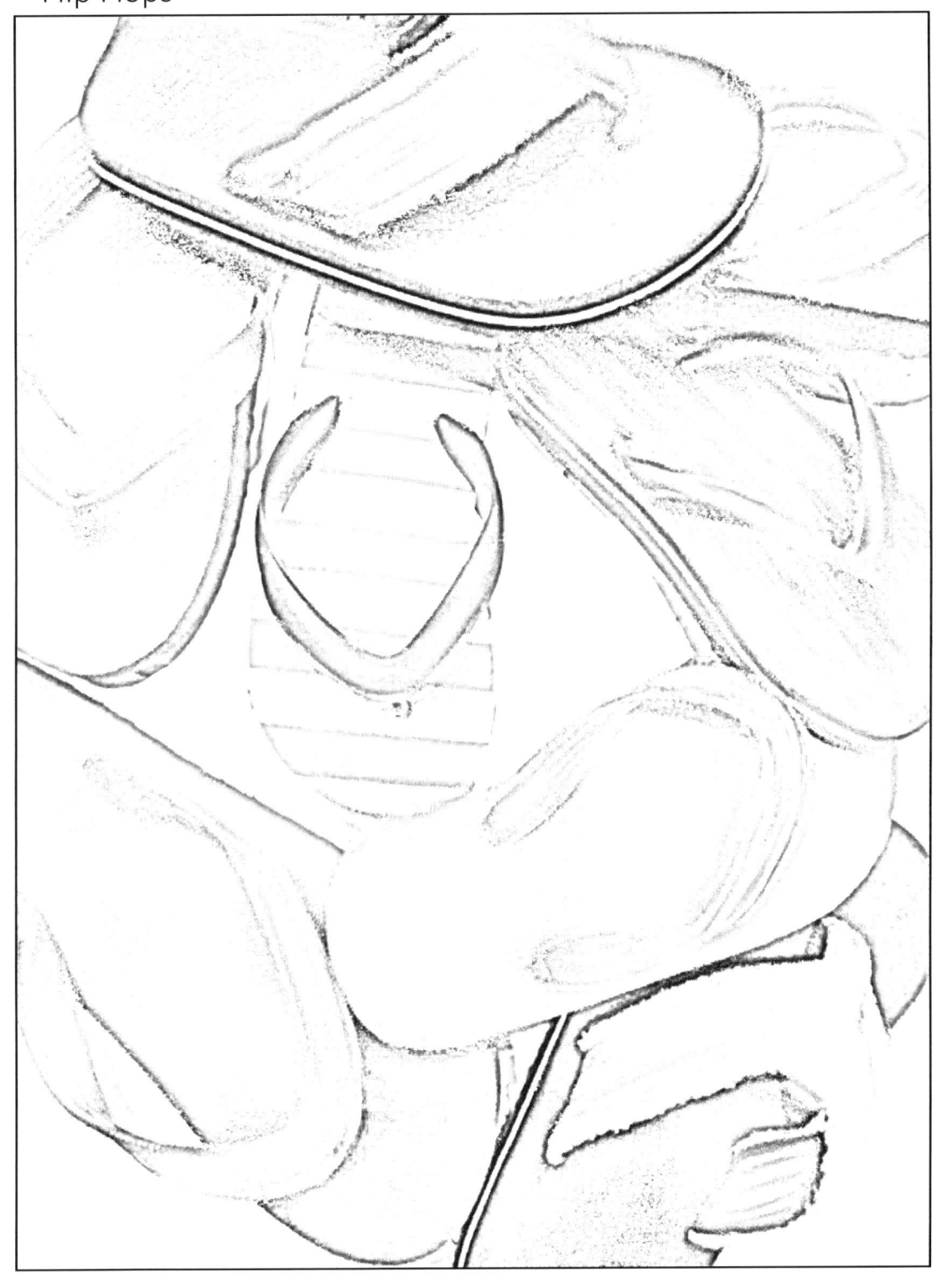

Footprints in the Sand

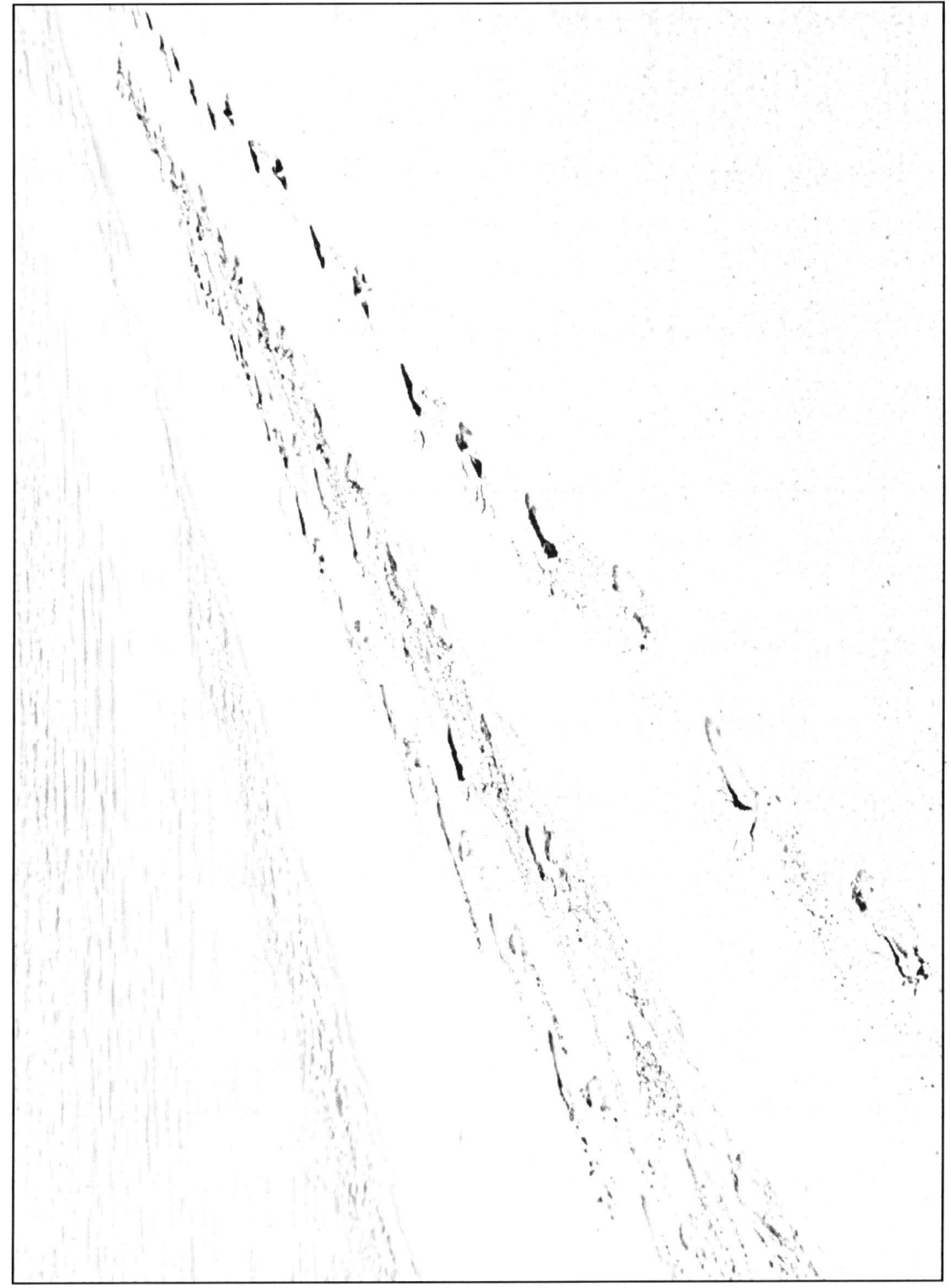

←

Jellyfish

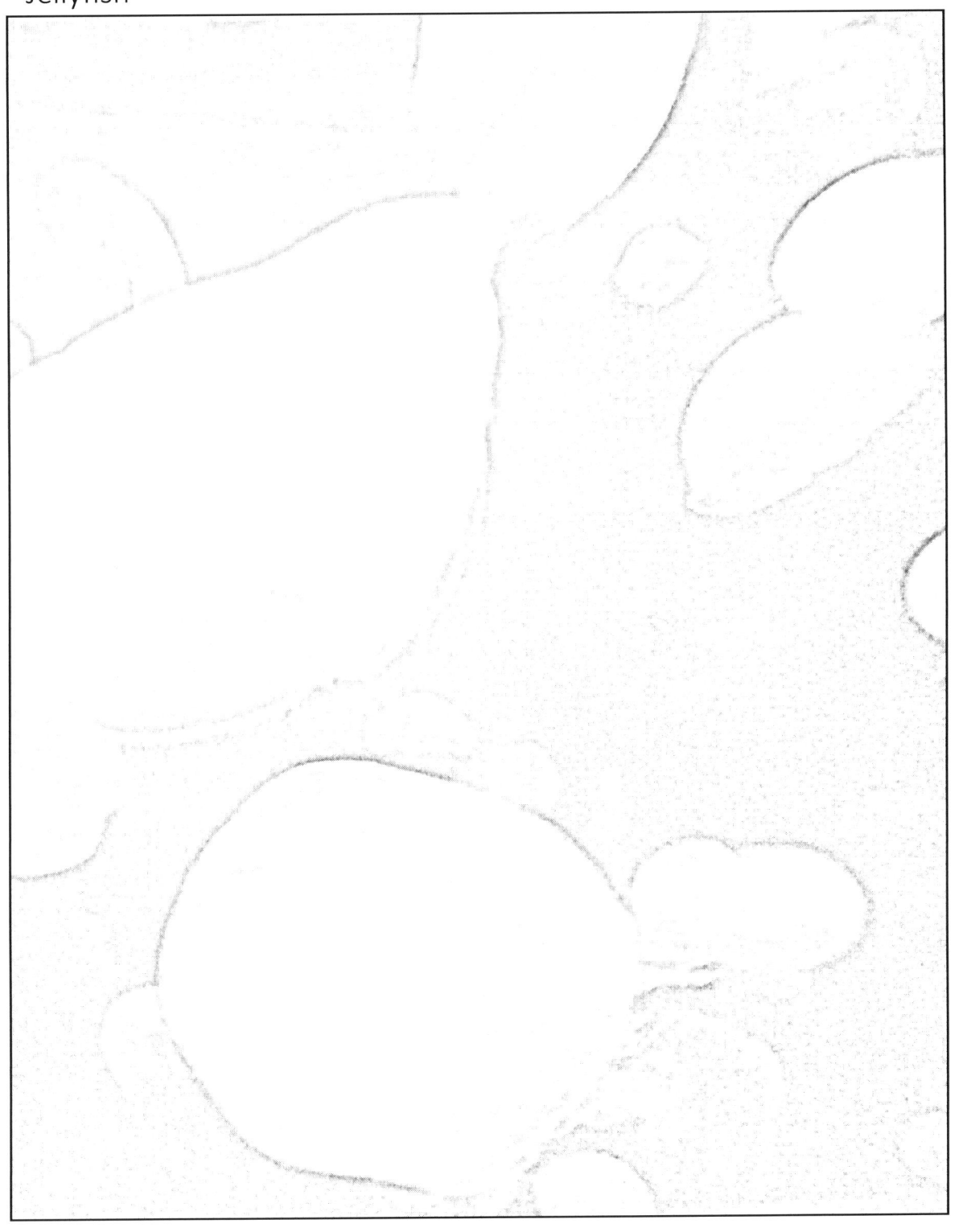

Masks and Snorkels

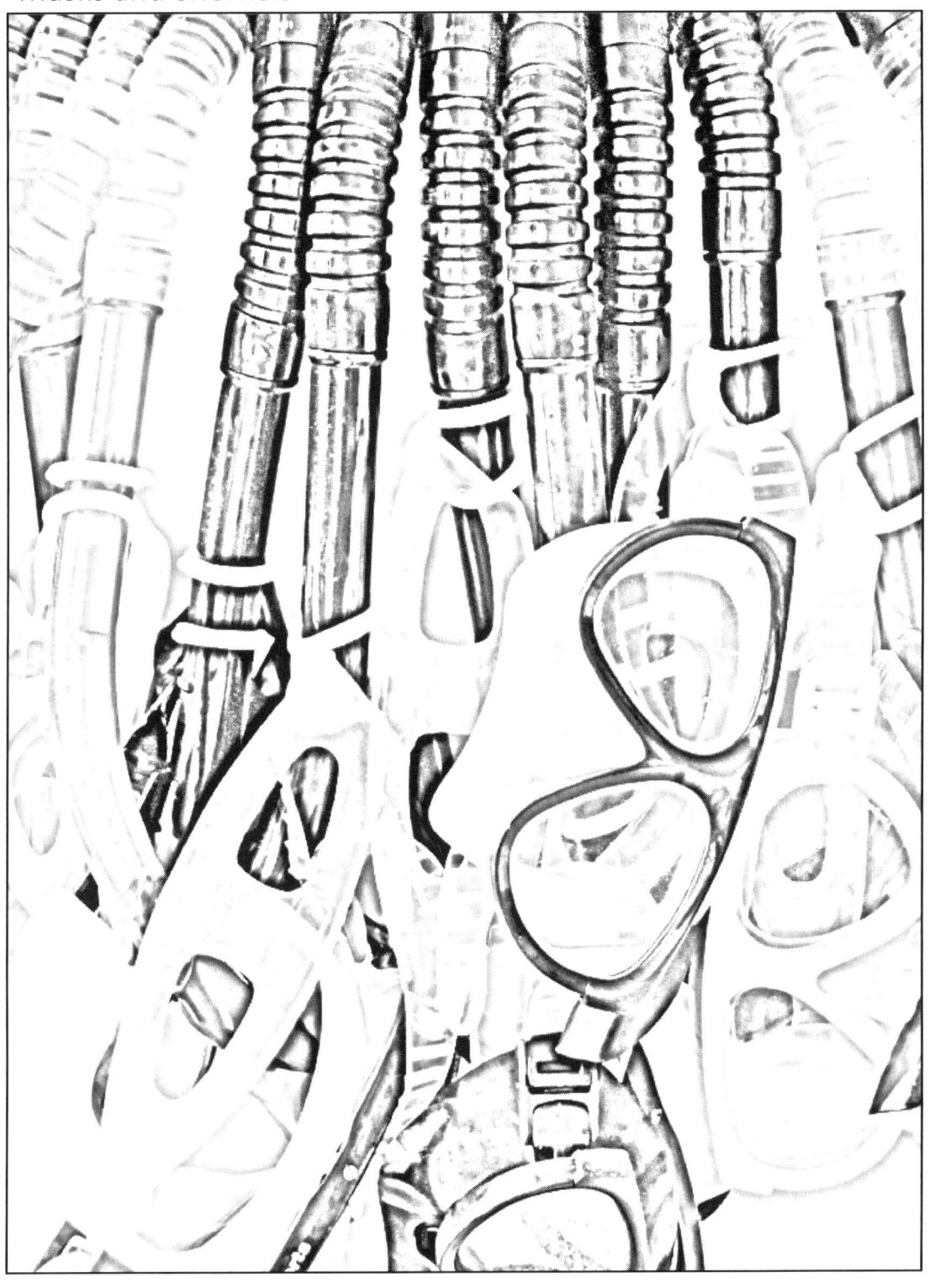

Noodles

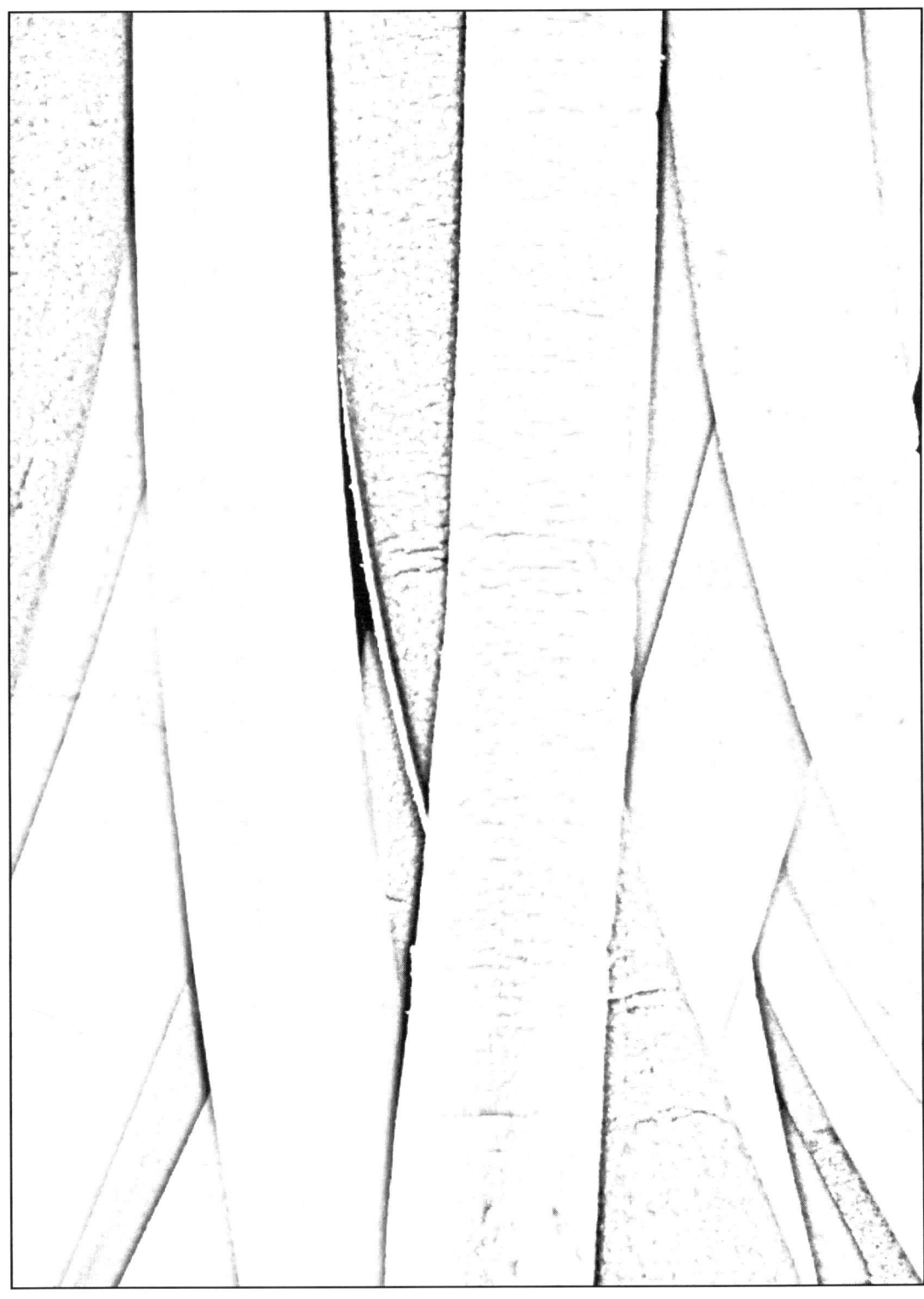

Palm Trees

Pelicans

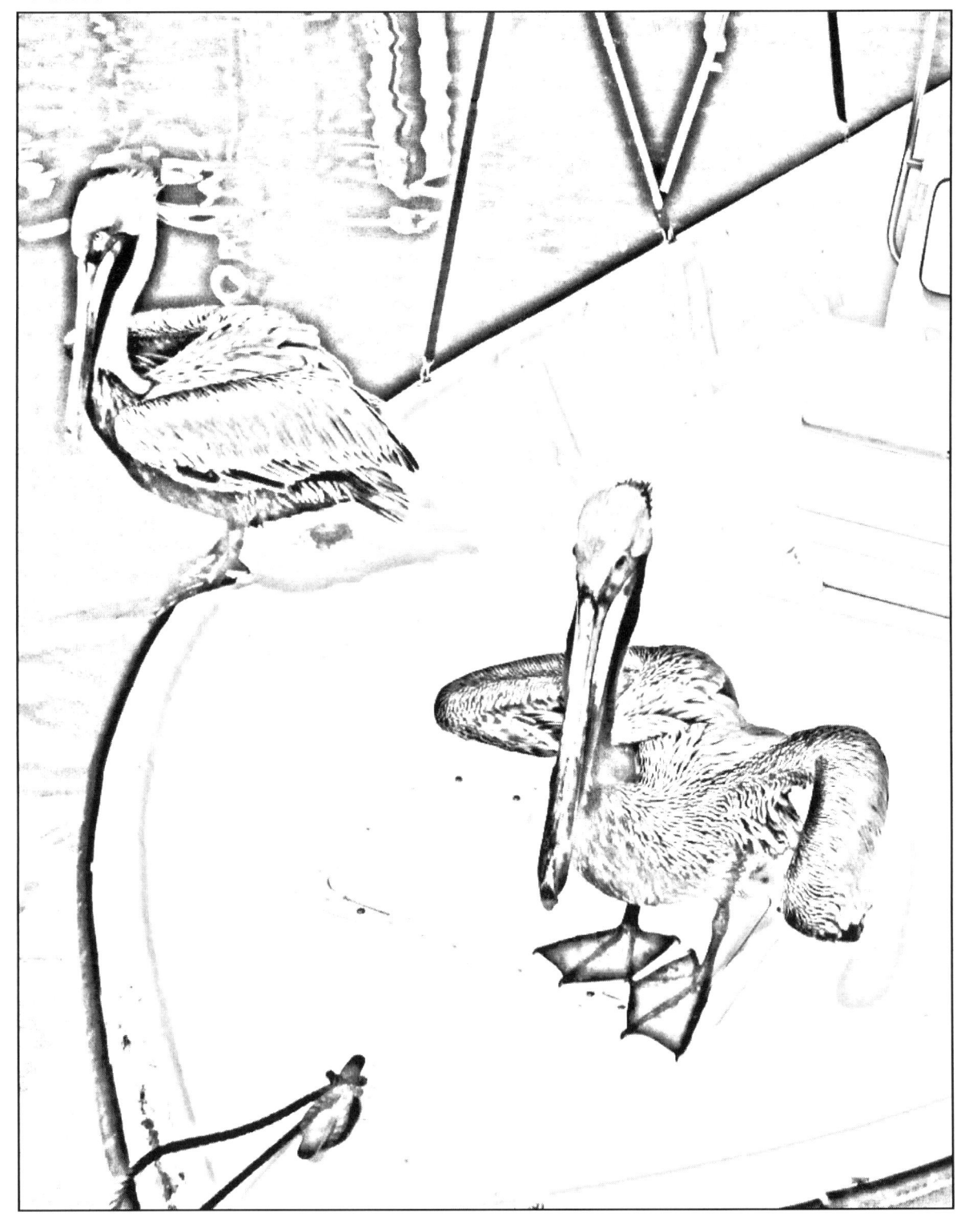

Sand Dollars

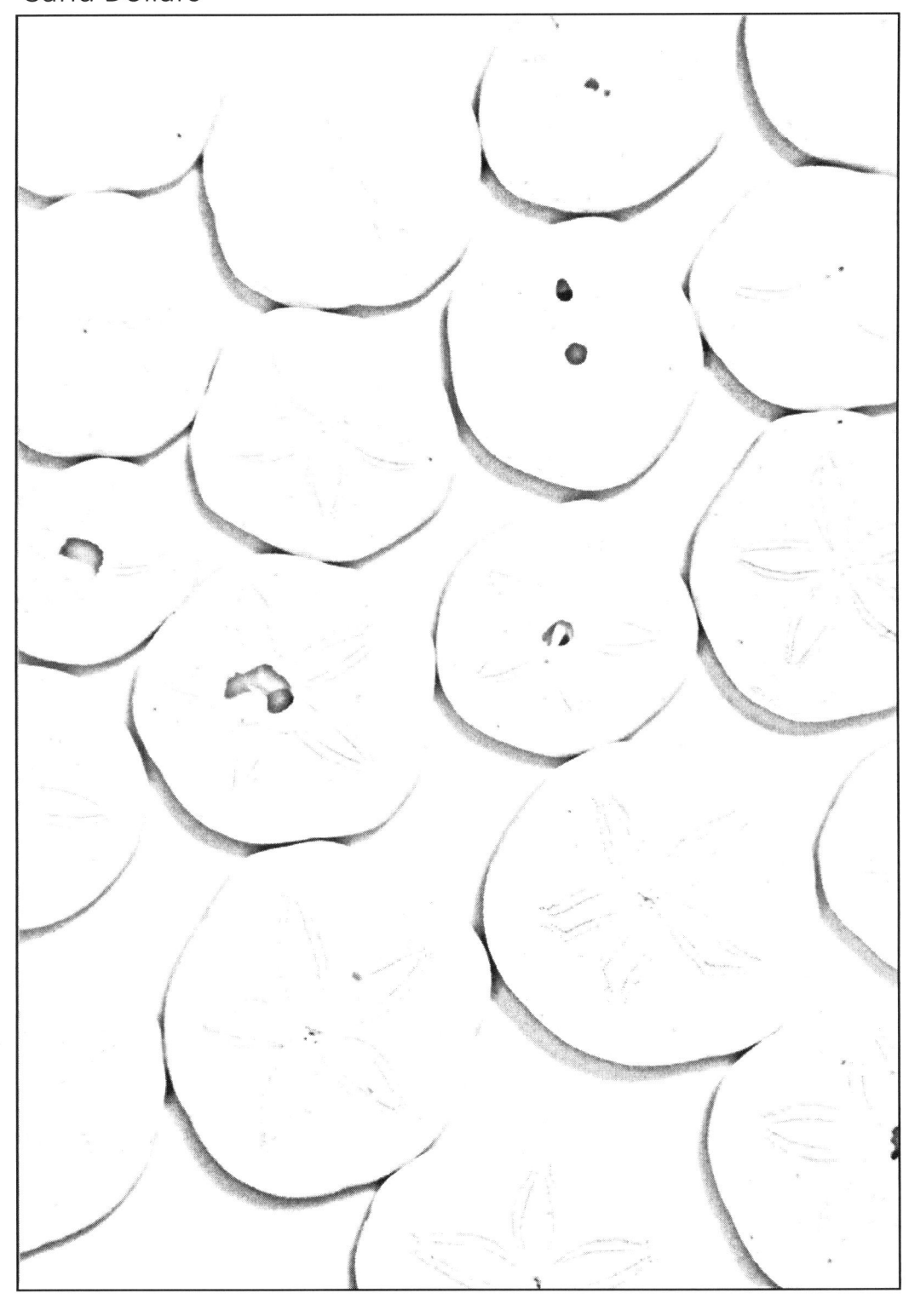

Sand Toys

Sand

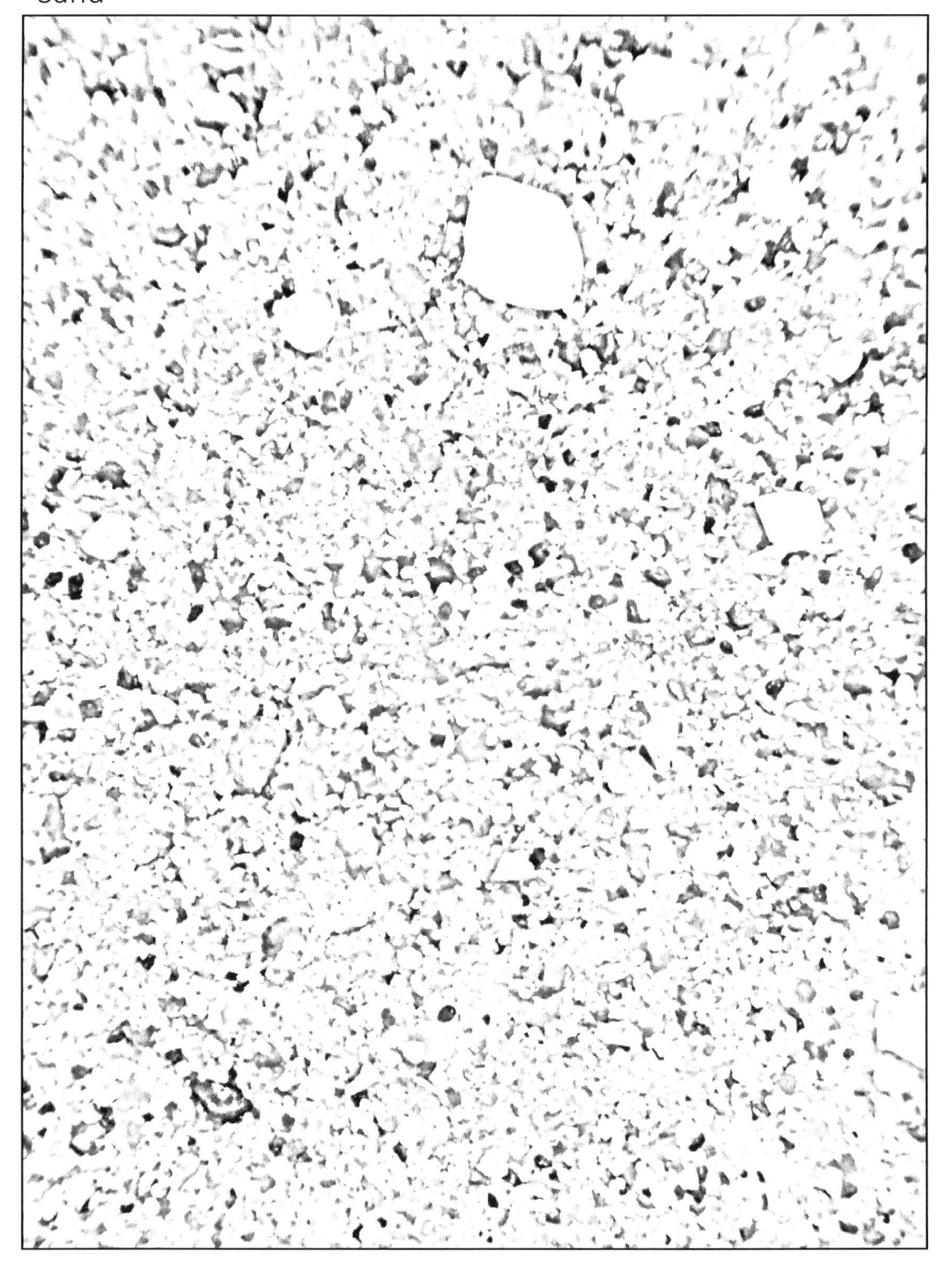

School of Fish

Seashells

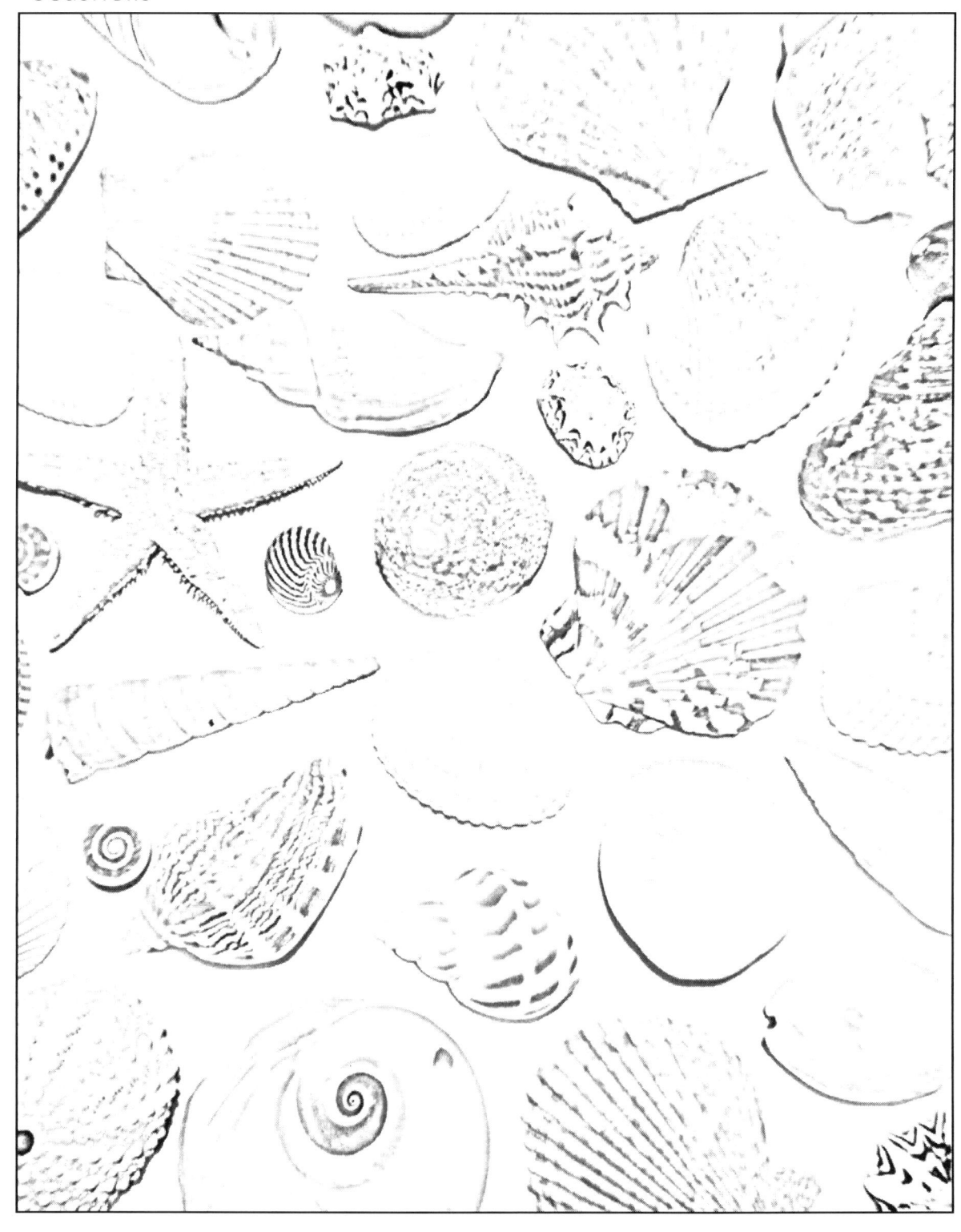

Starfish

Sunglasses

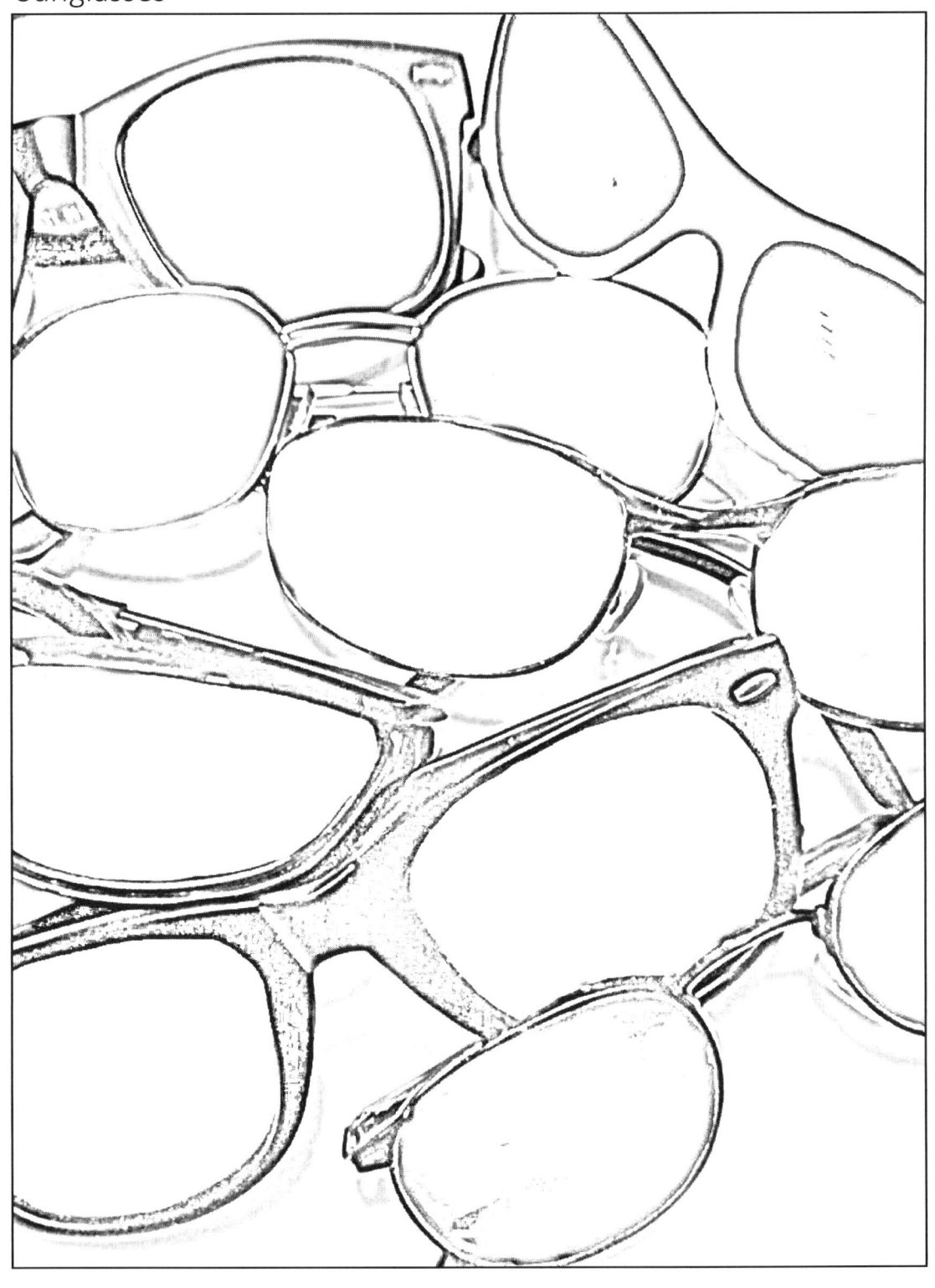

Sunken Ship

Sunset

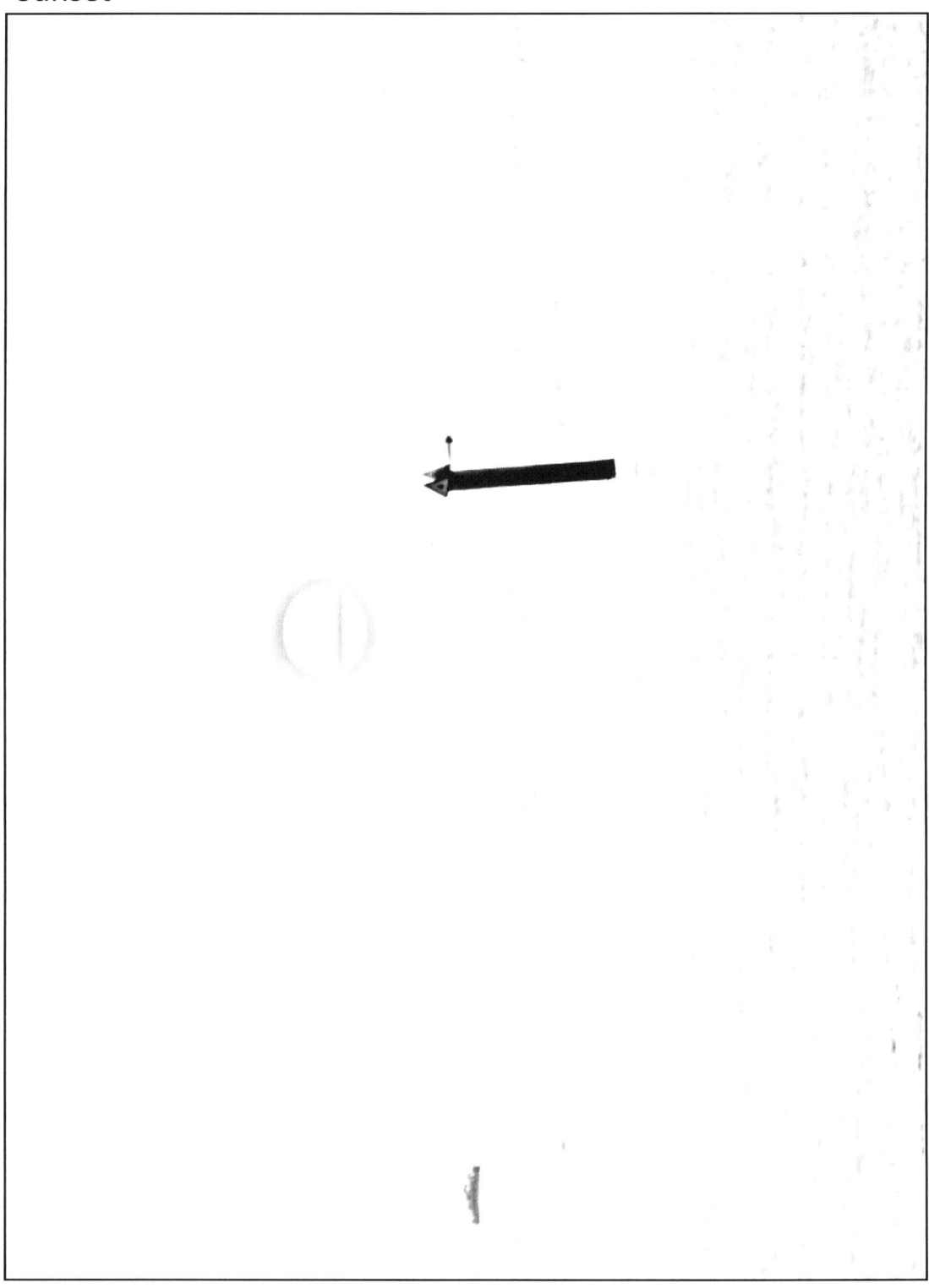

Suntan Lotion

Swim Trunks

Water Bottles

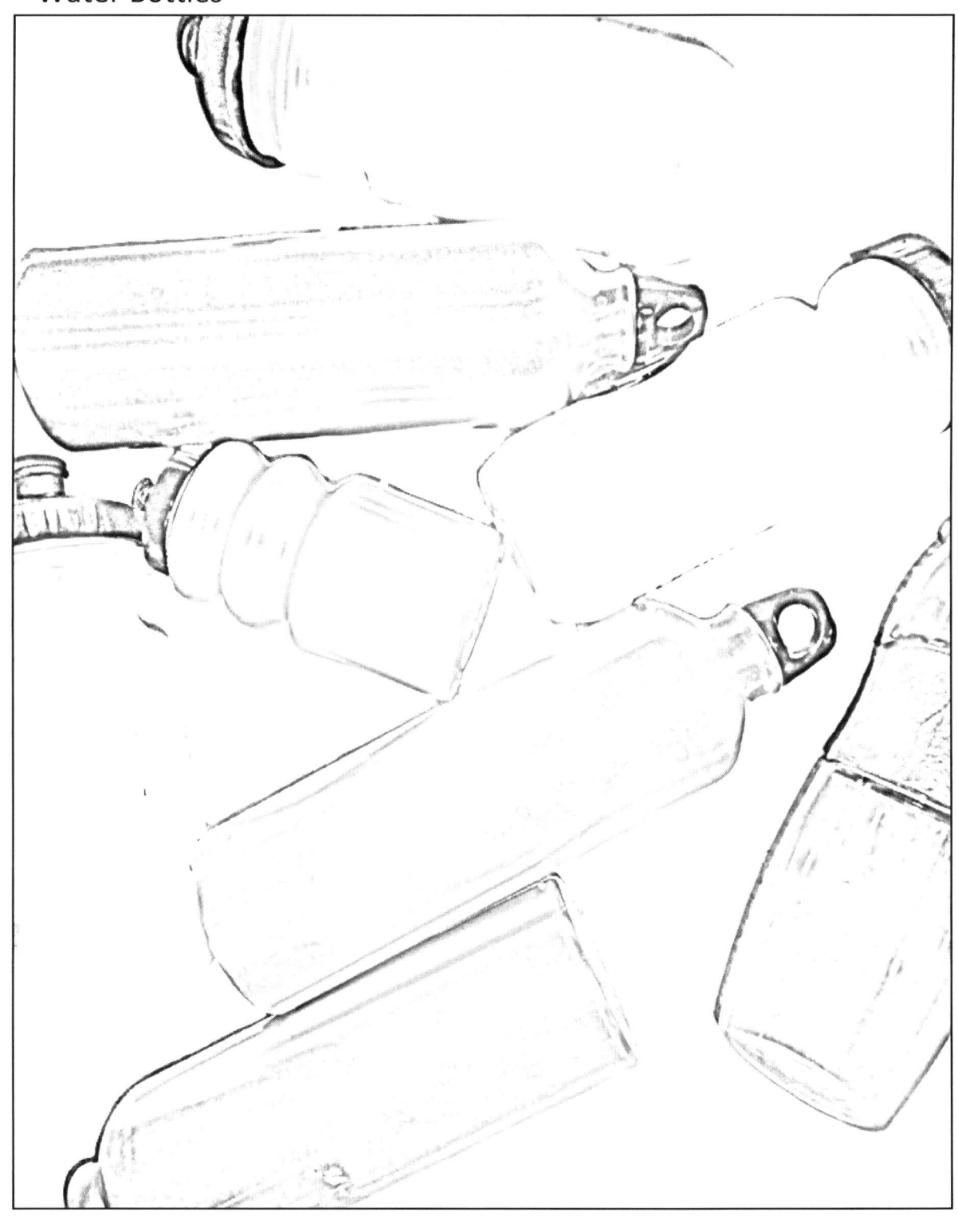

Made in the USA
Middletown, DE
19 December 2015